another season spent

Richard Allen Anderson

Vabella Publishing
P.O. Box 1052
Carrollton, Georgia 30112
www.vabella.com

©Copyright 2013 Richard Anderson

All rights reserved. No part of the book may be reproduced or utilized in any form or by any means without permission in writing from the author. All requests should be addressed to the publisher.

Manufactured in the United States of America

13-digit ISBN 978-1-938230-27-1

Library of Congress Control Number 2013900252

10 9 8 7 6 5 4 3 2 1

DEDICATION

To all those who have gone before—
contributing untold works
of wisdom and beauty,
and to all those who will follow—
may these pages hold for you
some measures of beauty and truth
or merely
prompt a chuckle, a smile, a tear

and to Dolly

No Ordinary Fish

I caught a fish the other day.

Glancing down I perceived it dimly
through rippled waters
wagging its tail at me.
Odd, I thought—this fish
acknowledges my presence
but does not dart into the depths.
And so I reached down
with my left hand and grasped it

expecting now for sure that it would
squirm away and leave me foolish,
empty handed.
But no, this cold creature did not
twist or fight as all fish do
when I lifted it dripping from the water
and held it in my two hands
beheld it face to face, dumbfounded.

This is no ordinary walleye, I said,
as the fish looked me in the eye
raised one brow quizzically and blew
me a fish kiss. Well I'll be damned!
So when it spoke I hardly flinched:

My name is Pythia, it said, through bubble lips
but you can call me Scales.
I have the answers you have been searching for.

The answers?

Yes. It flipped its tail impatiently.
So ask away, I haven't got all day.

But I don't know where to start.

So what?
You never did.

Then I pondered on the expanding universe,
(or is it universes in the plural)
and how it (or they) came to be.
What would I find beyond the outer edges
of the cosmos, of space and time? and
of the soul—its composition and mortality
the meaning of beauty
the need for evil
how life came to be
collisions of galaxies
the death of the sun
my parent's graves
my children's faces
my life
love.

The walleye pursed its lips
but with no other word
it shook its head
and shrugged.

I placed it deep down
into the water
a full arm's length.
I felt its scales abrade my hand
as it backed off slowly, and
with a sudden silvery burst
I saw it flash away.

No ordinary fish.

Table of Contents

Part One

Another Season Spent 3
Reverberations 4
Address Book 5
Scraps 6
Estate Sale 7
Transparency 9
Autumn Shadows 10
Assistants 11

haiku

sound of water 13
seventy nine 13
Avodart 13

autumn breeze 14
cold face 14
shadows 14

pretty pretty 15
cardinal calls 15

day upon day 16

Part Two

Conversation on Bluebirds...........................19
First Frost.......................................20
Fair Compensation................................22
Autumn Storm.....................................23
Foam 25
Reality..26
The Ages of Snow.................................27
Blue Heron Blues.................................28

<u>haiku</u>

thunder growls 29
spring rains....................................29
tinted clouds...................................29

black wings 30
titmouse..30

snow, snow......................................31

white morning 32
glacial blue....................................32

sweat 33
summer afternoon 33

lazy Saturday...................................34
sweet and spicy 34

Part Three

Ida 37
Brothers..39
Cave In 41
On Hearing It's a Boy 43
Mid Term 44
Impetus..45
Love, M...46
Touchstones 47

  haiku

ceiling fan...48
sparrow...48

they survive 49
we survive 49

unexpected 50
comfortable 50

mother's hands 51
only hope..51

Part Four

Fair Question 55
Ode to Toes 56
Gas Logs 57
How Do You Do? 58
Fall Back 59
April Anathema 61
Waiting Room 62
Pushing Out 63

 haiku

gesundheit 64
capital R 64
nos red na 64
faux pas 64

new shoes 65
morning pills 65
dinner time 65

Irish or Scotch 66
Saturday mass 66
Snowplow 66
Bologna 66

Part Five

Evanescent Reminiscence 69
Spring Rains 70
Whither Withered Wishes 72
But I Digress 73
Generations 74
Discovery 75
Take it From Me, Kid 77

  haiku

folded note 79
surprise! 79
emptiness 79

don't be angry 80
stroke 80

Father died 81
Mother died 81

mushroom cloud 82
questions 82

Part Six

The Race 85
To Our Fallen Heroes..............................86
Washington at Delaware Shore.................88
Funnel Cake 89
I Hear the World Singing.........................90
One Line Like Poe 92

  haiku

twisted words 93
telephone 93

Kate Smith 94
symphony...94
southern voices.......................................94

neurons banging 95
haiku..95
billiards poetry 95

Acknowledgements..................................96

Final Word 97

Enigma 98

Poem Index 99

Haiku Index 101

Part One

Another Season Spent

The taste of fall at last is on the season's lips.
Cool morning mist startles with its touch.
Faded summer blooms still greet my eye today
subdued and hesitant before they pass away.

Bright golden leaves shine through the shroud of fog—
shimmering droplets squeezed from the humid atmosphere
by temperatures well below the saturation point.

Another season spent.

A welcome passage after months of summer's heat
and yet, what new directions will the paths of autumn take
before the fallen leaves expose branches gray and bare?

And what of winter's coming?

REVERBERATIONS

Reverberate: 1. to force back. 2. to continue as in a series of echoes.

Waves wash gently on a distant shore
soft rain falls on the irises
the varied voice of nature conjures more
sequestered in my memory.

A small voice from the back seat of my car
sings Old MacDonald Had a Farm
spins off the two times tables, then
asks if I am older than the moon.

I hear the tiny sparrows chirp, content.
But have you heard their frightened fluttering
in the aviary purgatory
of the Kroger Store?

The poet's voice recites.
The mournful sax sings the blues.
Thunder shakes the windows in the night
and I hear her breathing next to me, asleep.

I hear her call my name with crackled tones
fractured by relentless time, and yet
Puccini's Butterfly has never sung
a sweeter aria for me.

Now take the babies from the crying room.
Let them murmur, gurgle, howl and wail
at the strange proceedings,
the ancient hymns and rites.

There will be time enough for silence.

Address Book

A ragged paperback,
four and a half by seven, divided alphabetically
with space for names, addresses and telephone numbers,
a palimpsest of frequent change, notes and cruel cancellations.

Some faded entries,
used for regular communication
or even just at special times,
come readily to memory's recall.

With others, we take some moments pause
to think—now who on earth was that?
Too many are neglected and unused.

Marginal reminders on scarred and blemished pages
signal bridges and crossroads—the Rubicons of Life—
birthdays, anniversaries, weddings and divorce.

Turning page to tattered page
a special sign appears, prompting
a quiet utterance or a sharp intake of breath—
the thin and poignant pencil line that deletes
without erasing: *out of service, due to death.*

Or we might laugh.
"We should replace this book, this paleography,"
we say, "start a fresh one, clean and new."
Then slowly, like the reluctant fading of the light
at eventide, we fold the covers closed, once more.

Scraps

You hoard your scraps of memory
in albums packed with fading photographs
on pages filled with scribbled anecdotes
of friends and kin long gone
whose existence now depends
on your ability and will to remember them.

Your fragile taped recordings hiss
and snap their aged essence, yet
recall with crystalline perfection
that single golden moment from the distant past.

You may resuscitate the failing media,
transform the images on film into JPGs on compact discs
save the written words as DOCs on DVDs
convert the tapes to MP3 stored in flash memory,
striving, struggling to prevent additional erosion
of the once-fresh passions
only your own mind is able to preserve.

Do not fret and sweat, old man.
Do not waste your time
on these vain frivolities.

The future will have memories of its own
and care not for your scraps of history.
Then hold them dear within your time
within your mind, within your heart
until they die or fly away.

Estate Sale

The hulking, rusted dumpster sprawls its length and width
filling the driveway, unbalancing the neat, stone residence
that now stands uninhabited after its final disembowelment.

They come from miles around, creeping their pickup trucks
and minivans over the crest of the street, parking
  helter-skelter
on lawns, in drives, cramming the street, seeking
  the bargain of a lifetime.

Treasures of two lifetimes intertwined, gathering
  and sharing,
some recent, some vintage, requiring even practiced
  hunters to question
What is this thing . . . oh, could it be? . . . and then
  move on, amused.

Jake died not long ago. He'd suffered long enough.

We thought to ask the widow, Oh Mary, can you come
for dinner with us sometime soon? but somehow never did.
Now she's gone too, and her little yipping dog.

Not dead, but in a home somewhere close to kin
after traveling by car to a family reunion that no one else
  attended
and driving off the road, bewildered but determined on a
  different occasion.

The last few items from the past are hauled up to the lawn
and stand like silent sentries next to the ReMax sign,
  looking out,
a dusty pair of upholstered rocking chairs with wooden
  arms
rocking together gently in the sultry evening breeze
looking toward the dumpster, brimming now
with its jumbled hoard of rejected treasure,
no longer needed, no longer wanted.

Transparency

*Transparency: A picture on film
viewed by light shining through*

Time has not spared the once clear and vibrant colors
now degraded to a monochrome magenta.
Unkind shadows undermine this photograph
of hauntingly familiar faces that strangers
would not recognize to be our very own.

Memory at once restores
the aged and long sequestered image
that yet has power to erase the toll of passing years.
Oh, how sharply does the heart recall
the essence of this sadly altered record of the past.

Look here! My senses all ignite
reliving now that isolated distant moment—
I smell the fragrance from the small bouquet she holds.
I feel the whistling wind that chilled her cheek
and ruff'd her waves of soft brown hair,
the touch of her small hand in mine
the electric moment when our lips meet, tenderly.

I hear the quiet, whispered words of love.
I am smitten now twice harder
than even in that fragment of time
we held together long ago.
I love more deeply now in retrospect
more constant in my mind and heart
than this muted vestige of our youth.

Autumn Shadows

Does the summer rose smell as sweet as this
 autumn flowering?
Was its form and color as perfect as this final
 single bloom?
Has the season of transition enhanced the blossom's beauty
or is my melancholy appreciation spurred and
 heightened by
unwelcome certainty that this too will soon fade away?

The planet spins, and day by day
contracting hours contrive a glorious blemishing.
Nature's chromophoric metamorphosis
transforms the verdant leafy landscape—
a dappling first, then golden clouds and red.

The falling leaves float earthward
to shrivel and die upon the ground.
Then stirs in me some late awakening—
a formidable phantom of unrest, hidden in the
 autumn shadows, waiting . . .
waiting for the cold calm snows of winter to descend.

Assistants

Elastic band around my knee
trifocals to help me see
amplifiers in each ear
more assistants every year.

Implants fill in gaps and spaces;
bridges span some other places.
New orthotics for my feet;
running shoes are obsolete.

Therapy may ease the strain
on aching joints swelled with pain,
or Dr. Daniels may help out
but might bring on a bout of gout.

I think that Old Number Seven
no doubt is a gift from heaven,
grain enhanced by fermentation
balm to millions across the nation.

I'm grateful when analgesics
squeeze the hurt till it ceases.
Blessed aspirin, Motrin and the rest
NSAIDs really do it best.

Now I notice more and more
folks seem inclined to hold the door
when I enter or when I leave—
is "Needs Help" written on my sleeve?

I'd rush to help not long ago,
now it seems I'm just too slow
mumbling my appreciation
unhappy with the situation.

I know those young folks all mean well
and truly pleased that I can tell
of the fine assistance that I get
. . . and yet . . . and yet . . . and yet.

haiku

the sound of water
gurgling in the fountain
makes me want to pee

seventy-nine
an old sonofabitch, a
geezer with a limp . . .

Avodart each day
attempting to appease
the prostate god

autumn breeze
swirling fallen leaves
letters from old friends

cold immobile face
pillowed in white satin
a vacant bird's nest

shadows on gravestones
gray thunderclouds gathering
I knew these people

pretty pretty bird
five notes float through barren trees
writing an old friend

a cardinal calls
alone and far away
signing divorce papers

day upon day
tiny moments piling up
smothering, killing

Part two

Conversation On Bluebirds

Hey, Come look!

What is it?

So rare, like never—
    the tree full of bluebirds sleeping.

Okay, I'll get the camera—
    Oh damn! I need to load some film.

Hurry then, they're waking in the morning sun.

The light's just right. I'm ready. Show me where.

There, right there. Look! Quick!
    Some are leaving now, already.

I'll just focus and adjust the lens.
See those two huddle side-by-side—
    Oh God they're beautiful.
All right, they're on my camera screen,
    I just need to push the shutter . . . .

Oh my. The last have flown away.
    Look at me—I'm tingling.

I suppose they were thrilling. Do you think
    they will return?

    Photograph the tree.

First Frost

No morning flutter,
leaf or wing.
The hopeful feeder
stands abandoned.

The birds puffed-up
in twiggy sanctuaries
reluctant to test
the thin and frigid,
early sun-streaked air—
to reclaim their heritage—
to fly
for food
or joy alone.

Surely one
famished or foolhardy
black-capped Chickadee
rust-flanked, crested Titmouse
or nervous, flitting, earthy Wren
will soon find courage
or compulsion to lead
into the still, chill atmosphere.

Silent companions
to the silver-frosted feeder:
yellow pansies in hanging pots
with drooping heads and lowered eyes
and I behind the glass
wait expectantly.
Watching.
Impatient.
Uptight.
Hopeful.

One welcome wren—
not nervous after all—
arrives at last.
I am relieved for my important daily tasks.

Fair Compensation

If I were a gardener by trade
each day before dawn dispelled night
I would rise from the warmth of
my bed and pull on a fresh laundered
pair of old pants that still held the
scent of the earth.

If I were a gardener, I'd know
from the feel and the smell of the
air at the window what manner
and weight of jacket or shirt
I'd don for the day to be spent
at planting or harvest.

Nature and weather would be
my hard bosses, strictly directing
the work of the day. I would toil
in the ground, on the branch, or at my
round table with pencil and notebook
when hard rains came.

My gardener skills would presume
to improve on Nature's designs
pruning odd branches and plucking weeds out
amazed by the beauty of each fair green child
mourning the death of another I'd held
with black-tipped fingers.

If I were a gardener by trade
my fair compensation would be
delicate smells and grand beauty
the small furtive bird, the bright flowered tree
old Sol who shines warm on my back
even dollars.

Autumn Storm

The storm came late last night.
Flashing
Crackling
Grumbling
War game noises
Majestic cannon music of clashing fronts
Shaking us half conscious
Chilling
Thrilling surreptitiously

Tat-a-tat-tat. Shake, rattle and roll.
Fat hard raindrops splattering windows
Drumming overhead
Hammering shingles
Like a mad roofer.

Beneath the comforter
Huddled like twin fetuses
We touched and held each other.
Half dreaming
Not awake enough
Nor brave enough to confront the tempest—
Tall trees twisting, resisting the furor
Growling and roaring
Just outside.

At morning's light crippled branches, stripped and stark,
point dark accusing fingers randomly on high.
The unconcerned gray sky rolls on
sends down stuttered smatterings
reminders of the nocturnal deluge,
warnings against indifferent egress.

Sodden autumn leaves unmoving in the wintry gusts
adhere like frightened children to the bleeding mother earth
a colorful patchwork, blurred through the mist-clouded window.
"What a night."
"Was there any damage?"
"I'll go out later to check."
From the television news we learn
tornadoes ripped the country.
Thirty-six perished.

Foam

The brutal north wind
prods with boney icicle fingers
pummels my body with brumal fists
buffets and beats without quarter
tearing the surface of the land and the sea
driving sand and salt spray onto my lips
into my nostrils.

Churning green breakers
spend their suicidal fervor upon the shore
spewing mounds of stiff sea froth at the water's edge
gray apparitions emerging from the sea.

Whirling outriders of the tyrant wind
rip reticent chunks from the huddled heap
scattering, propelling them across the glistening sand
skittering and darting in erratic dance
like legless ghosts of nervous sea crabs
seeking nothing, slowly diminishing, diminishing

vanishing.
Metamorphosis.
Transition into phantom vapor.
No trace remains

A black-hooded gull with broken-back wings
does air acrobatics, mocking the tempest
with shrieks of shrill laughter.

Reality

The morning air is gentle
sweet to smell after last night's rain.

The new moon
rides high above the treetops
pale in the still paler dawning sky.

Late autumn leaves,
splashes of impressionistic color
on scrawny, dark gray limbs, infuse
fire and russet tones
into the forest scene.

Scraps of gold-hued clouds
glide smoothly eastward
highlighted by the waking sun
avoiding the horns of the crescent
scattered by the subtle breeze
in one slow magic moment . . . they vanish.

I am alone.

Stillness arrests me.
Involuntary wonder holds me rapt.
A primordial thrill warms my guts
stirring my soul with unfettered emotion.

A fluttering wing or shifting shadow
dispels the moment, like the morning clouds.
My mind returns to focus, plan and analyze,
morning peace absorbed into an alternative reality.

The Ages of Snow

In frigid January
light breezes swirl the snow.
Fluffy, frivolous and airy
in temperatures of five below
it drifts to pile at fences
before the winds of night—
then amazes all our senses
with the new aurora's light.

In the slow return of morning
it lies quiet on the ground,
its stillness makes no warning
as it muffles every sound.
Bestowing calm and wonderment
it spreads soft beneath our sight;
the landscape flows mellifluent
all over hushed and white.

March brings sticky snowfalls.
They drop heavy and profoundly—
good packing for hard snowballs,
and snowmen stacked rotundly.
Children try to catch snow's coldness
on open palm and lifted face
they watch the crystal essence
morph into a liquid trace.

Groaning loudly under foot or ski
snow complies to hard compaction
warning town-folk to drive carefully
to be wary of uncertain traction.
Then shoveling is a murderous thing
torturing will and sacroiliac,
relieved but by thoughts that joyous spring
will soon come rushing warmly back.

Blue Heron Blues

The great blue heron
snaked his neck around
and winked his golden eye.
(I swear he winked at me.)
His spindle legs
pushed like springs, and
he rose up toward the sky.
(He did it leisurely.)

Wide-spread gray wings
flapped silently—
magnificence in flight.
His pointed dagger beak
pierced through the air
—a truly awesome sight.
Then I ran to check our pond
from whence the great bird flew.

He'd cleaned it out completely—
no fish remained, not even just a few.
His snack has cost me dearly.
(Koi dinners run about
twelve bucks per ounce.)
But not so much
as those poor fish paid
with all that really counts.

haiku

thunder growls threaten
lightning streaks a blackened sky
not a drop of rain

spring rains return
more softly than memories
of lost loves

scraps of tinted clouds
drifting in the dawning sky
no rain again today

black wings at gray dawn
silent against the pale moon
chill air frosts my breath

reticent titmouse
lured to the backyard feeder
finds a gourmet meal

snow snow snow snow
big white juicy flakes
will it ever end?

snow through the night
quietly descending
hushed white morning

glacial blue ice gleams
compressed crystals cleave and weep
free at last

a drop of sweat falls
upon the wilted roses
August afternoon

summer afternoon
children in a crowded pool
tadpoles with legs

lazy Saturday
leisurely loving
wet grass on bare feet

sweet and spicy
savory combination
kitchen or bedroom

Part Three

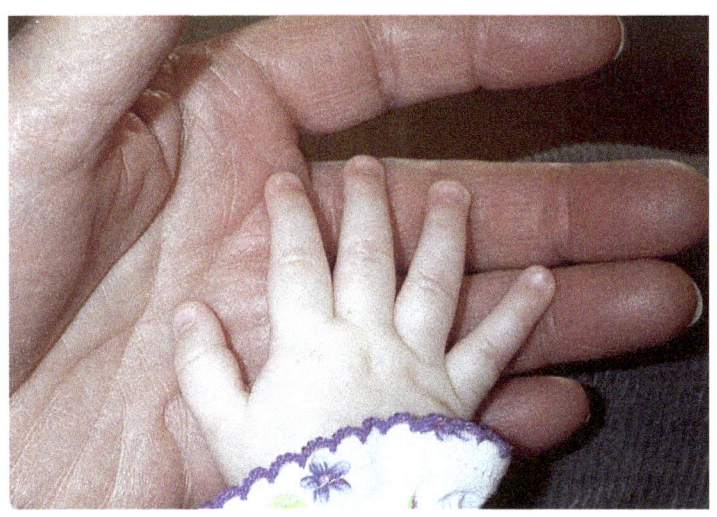

Hand of God Statue
by Carl Milles
Millesgarden, Sweden

Her Name Was Ida

Nothing about Grandma was dainty
except what she created with her hands
strong, thick German fingers
stitching fine rosettes and lacy patterns
with colored threads on cloth
skills she learned as a young girl
then had little time to practice
until life's demands on her diminished.

One night when I was twelve, reading in bed
a Costain novel that could not be closed
she rose from her bed to come to chasten me
"It's late, turn off the light, go to sleep."
I replied, "okay,"
and turned another page.

Each time she came, padding down the hall
in her long nightgown with its ruffled neck
duty bound to secure my wellbeing
I'd say, "In a minute," or such.
But Costain's appeal was more compelling
than her discipline, so the book was finished.

Next morning she fixed breakfast
waited while I slept upstairs
and later watched in silence while I ate
unmindful and ungrateful
taking her for granted as I always did.
She was the kind one might take advantage of.

She sits erect, school-marmish,
a young woman uncertain of her self-worth
her distant gaze unreadable
slender and unsmiling as was the custom then
in a photograph with five others unknown to me
dressed in dark long-sleeved, high-necked satin
the fashion of the day.

I guess that she was married then
to George who disappeared one day soon after
or maybe just not long before.
And what was she to do alone
with seven children in her care?

She took it as it came
did what she had to do
with no greater expectations
from man or child or God.

The seven all survived
to spawn another generation
with Grandma's hands alone
to prod them, guide them, smooth their hair
they learned the value of a dollar and the truth.

Her name was Ida
plain and simple.

I still have a handkerchief or two
embroidered by her hands
with my initials
fine flowing letters
no stitch out of place.

Brothers

We are three brothers.

The youngest died at twenty-five
on a Florida highway drenched in rain
shrouded in early morning fog
driving to work to support his young family.
Brutally. Quickly, we all hoped,
when we viewed his mangled body.
That was years ago.

I told him tales when we were young
sitting on the edge of his bed at night
or in the morning light,
his eyes wide with wonderment
or at times with childish mirth
wrinkling his fair face.
His name is Edward.
We call him Buddy.

Brother Ron, the oldest, lives on too—
you may choose to call it that—
dying nodding in his wheelchair
hour by hour, day by day.
He does not know his child's face
or understand the woman
who visits now and then
is his wife of sixty years.

In the darkness
of his clouded brain
can he still see
the kites he built and flew
magnificent, swooping, soaring
responding to tugs of his hands on wires
flying but not free?

And I

Cave In

Darkness
Suddenly
Profoundly
Cool and Damp
Sharp Jagged Grits Pressing
on my body
on my face

Darkness
Immobility Compression Silence
I can't move!
I cannot breathe

Cool Darkness
Helplessness
Moments? Minutes?
Alone
in the Darkness
Then calm. No fear.

Voices
Ronnie's muffled shout
Mama's panicked words
Dickie. Oh No. Dickie . . .

Digging Scratching
Hands brushing smothering sand away
from my nostrils
To breathe again—Gulp Air Spit Sand
from my eyes
To see again—Daylight,
Gaping Mouths, Frightened Eyes
Frowns on Fearful Faces

from my neck and shoulders
To feel again the warmth of the sun

Pulled at last from granular confinement
limply into grateful arms
Rejoicing Admonitions Laughter
Dad says, "No Harm Done."

The voices and hands belong now to the past
the memory fragmented and faulty.

But you should know
I'll hurt you if you try to hold me down
I must know the exit's near

You must not stand between
Just let me know that you are here
By gentle touch or whispered name

Let me run free—
sun or rain upon my face
lungs filling and exhaling.

Let me see the light—
colors of the rainbow
in a clearing sky
birds in flight
sunset on the ocean.

Let me feel your warmth
whenever fear returns
again.

On Hearing "It's A Boy!"

"Ah ha"
I said,
uncertain,
listening closely to detect
tremors of joy or disappointment
in the mother's voice —

my daughter.
A mother now

The impatient life she proudly hosts
has sex, identity —
his image shown by ultrasound.

Restless, moving, racing heart
and tiny fists, 1.7 pounds they estimate.
God, keep them safe and whole.

...I was...really, rather hoping...for a girl.

Mid Term

A bulge
A mound
A protuberance
A growth
A belly
A gut

Round mound
Smooth Soft Firm
Fleshy protuberance
Round extended protuberance

Bulging belly
Growing belly
Growing bulging belly
Live and growing bulging belly

Moving mound
Moving growing mound
Miraculous moving mound
Warm miraculous moving mound

Touch
Gently touch
Touch and listen
Feel the miraculous moving mound

Life
Life in the gut
New miraculous life
With finger tips and ear pressed close

I feel it!
Shhhh! Listen!
Yes yes. I feel, I hear

Impetus

A favorite aunt
whose warmth and wit
has charmed for generations
one day departs from her familiar apartment door
to fetch the morning mail.
Confusion, fear and anger
well like swift black clouds in leaden skies
when feet and mind cannot retrace
that small journey home again.
"What's wrong with me?" she chides herself.

My older brother
still knows me on the phone,
my voice perhaps an echo of his own,
yet he forgets his recent breakfast menu
and later turns away to ask his wife,
"Hey, how old am I?"
"Nothing new here," he says.
He sounds serene.

At times a name familiar or dear will not be recalled
or the fastest shortcut through our small town's streets . . . .
Has that corrosive gene loosed its congealing acid
in my brain?
What sweet relief
when Alzheimer's cold and sunken eyes
are averted from my face again.
The name returns—Oh, Yes!
The route comes clear again.

I must hasten to complete my work
and go not gently to that dark fate.

Love, M.

She was our first

an easy child to love, adopted
after three months in an orphanage had left their mark
those months when compliance replaced self-confidence.

Three months of diapers overdue, her cries to no avail.
Three months to learn to hold a bottle propped up on a pillow
the Sisters in white too busy tending others in their charge.

She grew in beauty every year
twirled batons, her dark hair flying
spun melancholy airs from her silver flute,

yet joy stayed in the shadow of self-consciousness.
No cajolence or persuasion could
coax decisions from her lips,

Just pick one, white or black.
Which do you like? We don't care.
not knowing that she might prefer the blue or green . . .

She held steadfast behind dark eyes and
 a fragile wall of silence
or offered simply, I don't know, I don't know—
avoidance was her game.

We found her note
when we returned from a brief holiday away.
I'm eighteen now and I've moved out.

Come see me sometime. ~ Love, M.

Touchstones

Nearby, a couple walks
a shaded path, their hands entwined.
Decrepit memory recalls
electric surges to my youthful heart
and loins from fingers in a shy caress.

My grandson tugs
my stubbly beard and strokes
my laughing lips with baby kisses
on his fingertips, or probes an ear or watery eye,
then turns to place his tiny palm on mine.

As once I reached
for reassurance from
my parents' hands, so too my children sought
and found sweet safety from uncertainty
or fear. Small hands held out with total trust.

Dear friends have felt
the comfort of my touch—
these gnarled fingers holding theirs in times
of strife or sorrow. Strange, how hands convey
the deepest feelings our poor words confuse.

Her fine, strong fingers placed
a silver band on my left hand.
They thrill me still as even then,
with soothing soft unbidden touch that speaks
of years we've shared—and love, oh yes, of love.

I see
her wrinkled fingers now
compressed in childlike supplication
to her Lord that those she loves may
one day together hold the hand of God.

haiku

the ceiling fan
pushes uncertain currents
baby learns to blow

one tiny sparrow
hopping over crusted snow
our baby's first steps

fading photographs
they survive through remembrance
and forgetfulness

fading photographs
we survive through remembrance
and forgetfulness

unexpected smile
provokes my own—then I laugh
one small tooth missing

he is wool and she
cotton and polyester
worn, comfortable

laundry fluttering
wooden pins hold securely
my mother's hands

I could not pray
but only hope that I was wrong
when my parents died

Part four

Fair Question

Gulls swim.
Gulls fly.
Are the seagulls
smarter than I?

Ode to Toes

My southern-most appendages toil long
and silent hours encased in muffled blackness
sweating over their hard labors:
walking, running, stumbling, shuffling,
stretching, stomping, kicking, reaching, balancing
on tippy toes with no appreciation shown.

Still, their complaints are rare.
When duty calls they're there
waiting for me to sock it to 'em,
boot-up, and take off running
without even an "If you please"
until I bring them home at night

and loose them from their dark incarceration.
(I confess that I wear shoes only in public.)
Breath free you funny little foot fingers!
Wiggle, squirm, suck air, look around, relax.
Put your feet up. Scratch each other's backs.
Look how they smile at me.

A short massage, some fragrant powder
as I acknowledge each with solemn dignity:
The stability of Mrs. Big (who sometimes goes to market)
The determination of Mr. Small (what frightens him so?)
And the three pudgy in-betweens who
stay at home, eat roast beef or none at all.

My toes. I can always count on them.

Gas Logs

Just flick a switch; the fire starts. Blue flames
heat fiberglass logs and embers to a cheery glow.
No fuss.

No need to fell and cut and split
the oak or birch—or even pine.
No need to lay a tinder base
and coax reluctant tiny sparks to grow
into voracious teenagers, forever hungry and dissatisfied
until, all fiber, pitch and bark consumed,
only ash remains.

How Do You Do?

In our polite society
we find a great variety
of taboos, to-dos and no-nos
or things we just don't talk about.

George Carlin's bad vocabulary
damned by the constabulary
provoked glee or consternation
depending on one's point-of-view.

Even ordinary words and phrases
denoting common acts and places
may strain fragile sensibilities
if too overt or open.

Don't tell me if it's too revealing
I find it not the least appealing—
some queries, thoughts and conversations are
just too far off limits, even amongst friends.

Still, I have this burning question—
not that I require a lesson
or have some weird obsession—
so please forgive my inquiry:

But . . . do you fold or do you crumple
and do you use three sheets or two?

Fall Back

I have an extra hour today
to use as may occur to me.
Reprieve, reprise, or red-hot new—
what will my extra hour be?

It's a gift when daylight saving ends,
to throw away or keep.
Maybe I will read a book
or get some extra, needed sleep.

I have no plan to spend it well,
although I had fair warning.
One problem is—I cannot claim my gift
till two o'clock in the morning!

Set back the clock hands for one hour,
it should be automatic.
Yet, fulfilling all this encore time
is becoming problematic.

A list of chores looms now in mind,
un-started or undone.
Maybe I can use this hour
to list them, one by one.

Pad in hand and pencil poised
my vision's getting bleary,
just writing all these undone tasks
is making me so weary.

Maybe I should rest a bit.
Let's see what's on TV.
But now my clicker thumb grows sore,
I can't find anything to see.

I know what I can do
to commemorate this date!
I will write a clever, little poem—
but heck, now it is too late.

April Anathema

The taxman cometh each spring of the year
demanding cruel tribute. (For what? I'm not clear.)
I'll give up my share—but not one cent more—
enticing deductions like a skilled matador,
while crunching the numbers like a financier.

I'd read the 1040 instructions, oblique and austere,
completed all worksheets—incredibly queer,
plugged in numbers ten hours or more
till blood pressure readings staggered and soared
like the national debt. The taxman cometh!

Forms, schedules and records litter the floor—
one big I-R-S pain in the pos-ter-i-or.
Ignoring one detail would be cavalier,
Sure to be found by a tax scrutineer
sniffing deep in a mainframe like a Black Labrador.

The terrible deadline draws crucially near
and thoughts of an audit send shivers of fear.
Maybe I need some professional help
to fend off or deal with that Labrador's yelp
when April is here and the taxman cometh.

Waiting Room

Patients come, patients go—
but I must wait, reason unknown.
Time ticks by, each moment slow.

I've registered, comme il faut,
even winked at that nurse-crone.
Patients come, patients go.

No word. No sign. No way to know.
I grimace, grunt and loudly moan.
Time ticks by, each moment slow.

Now hunger and impatience grow,
innards flattened to the backbone.
Patients come, patients go.

What a damnable imbroglio!
with visions now of beef bourguignon.
Time ticks by, each moment slow.

A name is called—now what John Doe?
Not mine! I sink back with a groan.
Patients come, patients go.
Time ticks by, each moment slow.

Pushing Out

They fill my veins with happy juice
before consenting to turn me loose,
then push me out after surgery
to rest at home with my misery.

Not bad, not bad I start to think—
then a twinge here or there, now and then, makes me blink
and look around to be sure I can get
to the Extra-Strength Tylenol and Percocet.

"Drink," they instruct me, and drink I do.
"Keep up your strength." So I eat lightly too.
Then slowly I hobble to empty my bladder,
glad for that milestone—till the pain makes me sadder.

The cramps and the jabs and the pains now abate
but one bodily function seems alarmingly late.
I strain just to the point I think prudent to do,
and, Eureka, I've found it! the reticent poo.

A sigh of relief and a gasp of delight
push out the gloom of intestinal fright.
Life is good. Life is grand. Life is great. Life is Boss.
I'm so much more now for my much-welcomed loss.

haiku

strange and wonderful
what poetry is this?
haiku! Gesundheit.

capital R
sticks out a leg to support
its engorged brain

nos red na drah cir
richard anderson
spelled backwards

don't bring up
my faux pas, I prefer
to be deluded

new shoes
I cannot keep
from looking down

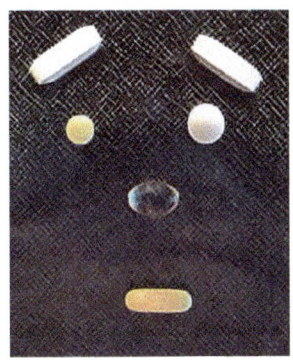

morning pills
enough to make
a funny face

dinner time
must we discuss
pubic hairs just now?

Irish or Scotch
or Tennessee mash bourbon
sunshine on my soul

Saturday mass
how wonderful to have
that chore completed

the cursed snowplow
pushes all my shoveling
back where it began

three politicians
stumping for reelection
bologna sandwich

Part five

Evanescent Reminiscence

A phantom cloaked in airy webs
stole unsummoned into my sleep
holding forth pleasure in one hand
grasping covert pain in the other.
She beckons me to follow
into the halls of shadowed memory.
She sings love's dulcet melody,
compelling my mind's eye to see
bright scenes of youthful reverie.

I run again, fast and free,
a stallion spirit, untamed, untried.
I shout and sing. So sweet is life.
Unbridled joy wells inside.
A girl with flowing hair and flashing eyes
walks toward me through the mist,
to hold my trembling hands in hers.
I kiss her shyly offered lips,
honeyed lips that welcome mine.

I embrace the thrill of new, unseasoned love.
We are one, alone in a world of strangers,
giving, taking, sharing what no others know—
for just a time, so brief a time until
the desperate grief of withering enchantment
pierces my young heart anew,
turning sweet words rancid in my mouth.
Oblivion returns like stealthy vapor
numbing each far recess of my mind.

With the dawning light I waken,
a tear still drying on my cheek.

Spring Rains

Strangers spinning time away
in a strange city on a Sunday afternoon in spring
our eyes compelled to meet across the empty tables
in a small café where few others dined, and then again
until at last I spoke.
Something quite meaningless, about the threat of rain
perhaps, or How was your salad? Mine had a bug in it.

Outside we met again, huddling, close as strangers may,
within the doorway's shelter from the soft, warm rain.
We walked together then along the fresh-washed streets.
From flowered branches, small birds
with their happy songs accompanied our chatter.
At last we came to her hotel.
I took her hand to say goodbye, but could not let it go.

We continued hand-in-hand,
waved at our reflections in shop windows
that each deserved our comments—
I'd love a shaggy coat like that, or
How much do you think that weird lamp costs?
At the park, we stopped to watch small children play
and laughed with them and spoke about ourselves
until we knew each other's lives in some detail.
Little there was we had in common,
and yet
we shared far more
than loneliness
sitting on a bench with gray clouds rolling by.

We wandered quietly a while, absorbed in private thoughts
or sometimes interrupting one another
as we started up again with more trivia
to share or just to mention one more time
that the afternoon had flown and dark was now upon us.

We watched and wished upon the stars spinning slowly
in their nightly journey across the velvet tapestry of night
and with the first faint light of dawn
we came again to the doors of her hotel.
Her kiss was soft and swift upon my lips.
Her scent remained, but she was gone—
gone.

I wonder,
when the spring rains come,
Does she ever think of me?

Whither Withered Wishes?

There was a time when I could fly
and dream of vast eternities
But now
I
sit
and
wait . . .

But I Digress

All of life is divagation
reckless wandering
squandering time
away
until
at last
our endeavors fail
to fulfill
the single sentence:
I am here because . . .

What more compulsion
must we seek
to assist a stranger
cause a child to laugh
or learn, or leave
a legacy of work
by which
some other
may conclude:
he was here because . . .

Generations

When leaves have fallen
shriveled, brown and speckled on the ground
a rose puts forth its final glory—
one bright, lonely blush, tall above the autumn tones.

Garden flowers give final burst
revived from summer's heat and thirst,
strong again but youthful not—
      take respite waiting winter's thrust

then yield at last—
not willingly—
grudging bequest
      to the generation next.

Discovery

I wish my muse had been
more compelling at the time
when all experiences was new
not covered with the rust and dust
and carrion of eighty years
or lacking that joyous intensity
of youthful, and even middle-aged,
discovery.

I was too busy then to heed her call
to write except on rare occasion
required by an English Teacher
in elementary school or even college
until those events that slapped me in the face
made me stop and sit bolt upright
amid the rush of life to pour
my soul upon the paper—
the new beginnings, the sorrowful finalities.

It may seem obvious to you
that writing of the past—one's own history—
is shooting fish in a barrel
compared to the fast-water casting about
for shadowy, silver aspirations
intimations of the future.
Well, it ain't.

More like deep water trolling:
Something is there, the muse insists
something in the murky depths
that needs to be brought to the surface
struggling and splashing
to be served up on a shiny plate
for all to taste and comment on.

I have never had much patience
for the uncertainties of fishing—
too busy living, loving, learning
seeking comprehension of the universe
to spend my hours in recollection
searching for some meaning in existence.

But the muse comes now more often to my side.
 "It's time," she says,
"You don't have forever.

Time has not tarnished your experience
but bestowed it with an aged patina
within some recess of your mind
turned and polished by life's labor
unheeded and unneeded until now
provoked by hunger for the truth
to abandon its dark sanctuary
to break its reticence
to express itself in words
to lead you to understanding.

 "Pick up the pen and book," she says
"your necromancers of discovery—write."
"Write!" she insists.
"Write for your life."

Take it From Me Kid

The once distant stranger now draws near.
At times I see his face,
wearing neither smile nor scowl,
so close at times, I feel his wintry breath
and hasten from the pale of his dark shadow.

Reluctantly perceiving the coming of that day when
the fear of light will overpower the fear of darkness
I pause infrequently from the meaningless travail
that offers no reward except for its completion,
to contemplate what meaning life may have,
as if it has some meaning beyond living.

It is the journey not the end:
the dripping of paint on canvas,
the lyric word that falls upon the page, magically
emerging from the murky, cluttered mind.

It is the singular golden memory:
delighted laughter of a child at play,
the tender joyful kiss of youth,
the wrinkled touch of aged love to say, "I know."

It is the rising, burning, setting of our sun over planet earth:
the perpetual daily struggle for growth and enlightenment.
At the end the page is blank again, the lessons lost,
engrained in my dust, dispersed throughout the universe,
indistinguishable.

Remember me then
when the subtle wind brushes softly on your cheek,
when musty autumn leaves rustle underfoot,
when good wine warms your gut,
when the poem sparks your mirth
or brings hot tears to suddenly wet eyes,
when the song gives your spirit wings,
when the butterfly kisses the bright white daisy,
when the first star glimmers in the evening sky. . .
for you are my immortality.

haiku

folded note
creases separating
one last look

surprise!
after more than sixty years
she should know him

first there was pain
time and seasons spun away
now just emptiness

please don't be angry
it's just that recently, I . . .
what were we saying?

stroke
urine runs freely—words fail
what is happening?

Father died alone
he had survived
previous attacks

Mother died alone
clutching her leukemia
gratefully?

mammoth mushroom cloud
beautifully cremating
Japanese babies

                              simple questions
                              alternative truths
                              many complications

Part six

The Race

Two sets of naked footprints
lead through sere and withered landscapes
leaving scarce impression on the crazed embankment
of the once fertile river bed

moving north, out of Africa
away from their uncertain origins
into their unknown nihilistic futures
driven by the force, the will to be.

Faltering but not failing
through pestilence and jeopardy
along an indeterminate unblazed trail
millennia on millennia

they walk side by side
over plains and mountain passes
stumbling through the ages
evolving progenitors of a ruthless race—

my ancestors.
Did they know love?

Whither shall my footprints lead?
What spoor or imprint might testify
to my existence fifty thousand years from now
or advance the wise-man species as those naked footprints did?

That long-distant future generation
looking forward, onward, outward
welcoming their modern ambiguities
perhaps on some far-off world or planet—

will they know their legacy?
Will they know love?

To Our Fallen Heroes

A teenage boy recalled for me
this homespun American tragedy.

He won't come home my momma cried,
and from her pain I knew—he'd died.

Dad's measured words flew back to me
—There's terrible work that I must do
to defend this country's liberty.
To make safe our world for Mom and you

I must leave our family and our home,
join those brave souls who will not yield
to freedom's threat. I'll not fight alone.
You'll be with me in each foreign field.

But I'll miss you Dad. I'm sure you know.
We need you here. Please, please don't go.

He looked at me with serious eyes
and held me close and tight.
—We will suffer bravely these goodbyes,
but we must be strong to fight.

It is a duty that none can shirk.
Some would destroy our way of life.
Toward that goal alone they work.
We must prevail and end the strife.

When your time comes to stand against
zealots and slavers and tyrant's threats
you too will come to our county's defense,
grateful to have lived with the world's best.

In every street, from every hill
let all with courage and conviction sing
for all to know the wellspring of our will:
Let freedom reign. Let Freedom Ring.

The boy stood erect; proud but sad
to honor his fallen hero dad.
He's not gone, he said, he lives in me.
He paid the price. No freedom's free.

Washington at the Delaware's Shore

This dark and frigid hour before the dawn
we steel ourselves with mighty, righteous prayer
to strike the redcoats unaware, perhaps
to gain a victory that sets our infant
country free. Our numbers small, we call
upon the advantage of surprise. Be still.

The fox attacks the lion in his lair
with stealth and cunning, seizing freedom's right.
We will avenge our suffering; long months
away from home and family. Long months
with hunger gnawing at our guts. Long months
of tyrant's threats to life and liberty.

We take our courage from adversity.
Remembering our wives, our kith and kin,
reject the awful, bitter winter freeze,
and warm our bodies and our souls with thoughts
of coming peace—tranquility. Be strong!
We hold the peace of Christmas in our hearts,

But first our war for liberty must start.
All men take up your arms and to the boats!
We cross the icy waters—quietly.
On Jersey's shores awaits our destiny!

Funnel Cake

Gray and haggard
A specter of a man
Hope struggling with Hunger in his red eyes
Approached the counter cautiously
To ask in quavering whisper
"Did someone leave that cake?"

I quickly intervened.
"It's mine."
And snatched my rightful purchase.

~

If only that lost moment might
Be relived. Revised.
No future kindness will erase
That hasty, thoughtless act
Nor divert his pitiful pained gaze
From haunting my mind, my soul.

What quarter
May I claim now
From all humanity?
Whose hunger torments now?

I Hear the World Singing

I hear the world singing in tongues
that are strange to my ear.

Those Chinese workers
building software and cell phones,
educated at Cal Tech and MIT,
Working harder, longer, cheaper. Making better.
Challenging the good old USA
they sing.

The Korean autoworkers sing in harmonious unison
but not in union.
Proud that Kias and Hyundais surpass
Damlier, Chrysler and GM in quality
they sing.

The Imam sings to bring his flock to prayer.
The oil-producing Arab sings on his way to the bank—
black gold, enough to drown America.

The Russian peasant sings a song by Emenem,
living in a two-room Moscow apartment
with two children and his chubby wife.

Illegal Mexican immigrants sing Hispanic melodies,
picking fields or nailing shingles
on roof tops across the country.
Twenty million strong.
Can you hear them sing?

America sings too.
Rival choruses, discordant, out of tune,
from the nation's capital
and from McDonald's drive-up window—
"Do you want fries, and can I upsize that for you?"
they sing
and go home to watch reality on their Japanese TV.

**Could I
but Write
One Line
Like Poe**

To my muse I mused
after reading poets
despised and dear,

Could I but write one line like Poe
I'd give of my life
one year.

She listened to me patiently
as I attempted to persuade her,
then turned and quickly walked away
from that uncertain wager.

haiku

my words returned
twisted corroded and bent
a knife in the heart

the telephone speaks
I am sorry to inform you . . .
deafening silence

Kate Smith stands and sings
No laser lights or fireworks
$E = mc^2$

symphony of life
drumming trilling discordant
looney tunes perhaps

southern voices
wet vowels and soft consonants
a cottonmouth strikes

neurons banging
synapses snapping
original thought

haiku haiku—it
pleases me to do haiku
concise flowing thoughts

billiards poetry
aimed to ricochet off the
cushions of your mind

Acknowledgements

Before I knew a single word, my mother read to me—poetry, stories, nursery rhymes—giving me a lifetime love of books and words. Thanks, Mom.

My dear friend, Adrian, read some of my earliest jottings as a mature adult in late life and encouraged me to become a writer. Thanks, Adrian.

Writing-club members, especially the Carrollton Creative Writers Club, have provided many profound critiques and much encouragement. My special thanks to Eleanor Wolfe Hoomes, Donna Spivey and Robert Covel for detailed comments on this manuscript.

Finally, thank you Dolly for always being my first reader and asking, "Where are all those poems; what will you do with them?"

Here they are.

Final Word to the Reader

Through these poems,
I share my most honest thoughts and feelings
with the hope you may come to know me
and perhaps, more thoroughly, yourself.

Richard Allen Anderson
Carrollton, Georgia
November 2012

Enigma

Footprints in the sand
and yet, no one has passed this way.
Could it be
I left them there
only yesterday?

Poem Index

Title	Part-Number
Address Book	1-3
Another Season Spent	1-1
April Anathema	4-6
Assistants	1-8
Autumn Shadows	1-7
Autumn Storm	2-4
Blue Heron Blues	2-8
Brothers	3-2
But I Digress	5-4
Cave In	3-3
Conversation on Bluebirds	2-1
Discovery	5-6
Enigma	Last Page
Estate Sale	1-5
Evanescent Reminiscence	5-1
Fair Compensation	2-3
Fair Question	4-1
Fall Back	4-5
First Frost	2-2
Foam	2-5
Funnel Cake	6-4
Gas Logs	4-3
Generations	5-5
How Do You Do?	4-4
I Hear the World Singing	6-5
Ida	3-1
Impetus	3-6
Love, M	3-7
Mid Term	3-5
No Ordinary Fish	Preface
Ode to Toes	4-2

Poem Index (continued)

Title	Part-Number
On Hearing It's a Boy	3-4
One Line Like Poe	6-6
Pushing Out	4-8
Reality	2-6
Reverations	1-2
Scraps	1-4
Spring Rains	5-2
Take It From Me Kid	5-7
The Ages of Snow	2-7
The Race	6-1
To Our Fallen Heroes	6-2
Touchstones	3-8
Transparency	1-6
Waiting Room	4-7
Washington at the Delaware's Shore	6-3
Whither Withered Wishes	5-3

Haiku Index

Clue Line	Part-Number
autumn breeze	1-4
avodart	1-3
billiards poetry	6-8
black wings	2-4
bologna	4-11
capital R	4-2
cardinal calls	1-8
ceiling fan	3-1
cold face	1-5
comfortable	3-6
day upon day	1-9
dinner time	4-7
don't be angry	5-4
emptiness	5-3
Father died	5-6
faux pas	4-4
folded note	5-1
gesundheit	4-1
glacial blue	2-8
haiku	6-7
Irish or Scotch	4-8
Kate Smith	6-3
lazy Saturday	2-11
morning pills	4-6
Mother died	5-7
mother's hands	3-7
mushroom cloud	5-8
neurons banging	6-6
new shoes	4-5
nos red na	4-3
only hope	3-8

Haiku Index (continued)

Clue Line	Part-Number
pretty pretty	1-7
questions	5-9
Saturday mass	4-9
seventy-nine	1-2
shadows	1-6
snow plow	4-10
snow snow	2-6
sound of water	1-1
southern voices	6-5
sparrow	3-2
spring rains	2-2
stroke	5-5
summer afternoon	2-10
surprise!	5-2
sweat	2-9
sweet and spicy	2-12
symphony	6-4
telephone	6-2
they survive	3-3
thunder growls	2-1
tinted clouds	2-3
titmouse	2-5
twisted words	6-1
unexpected	3-5
we survive	3-4
white morning	2-7

Notes

Notes

Notes